Chamber Music

by H. Voxman

for

THREE WOODWINDS, Vol. I

CONTENTS...

Rubank®

Hal•Leonard® CORPORATION

7777 W. BLUEMOUND RD. P.O. BOX 13819 MILWAUKEE, WI 53213

Scotch Quick-Step

Woodwind Trio

BEETHOVEN

Romance

Woodwind Trio

SPERGER

Ballo

Woodwind Trio

HANDEL

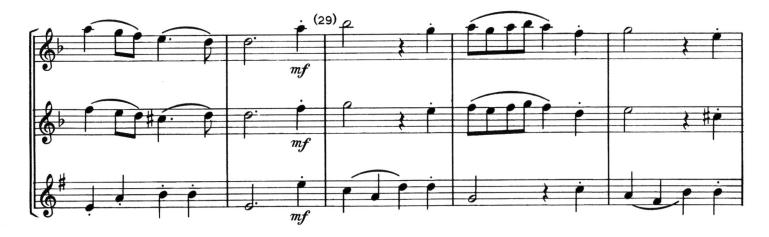

Three American Folk Songs

Woodwind Trio

Compiled and Arranged by
PAUL KOEPKE

THE BLUE-TAIL FLY
(5)

PETER GRAY

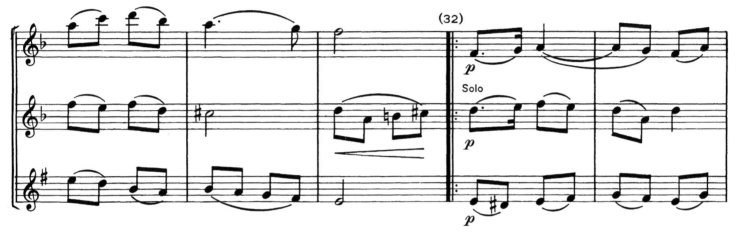

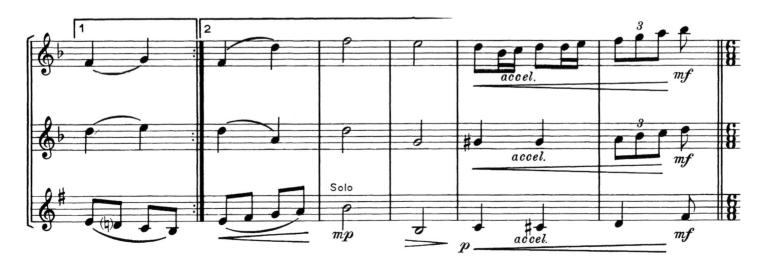

THE RIO GRANDE

Adagio
(Divertimento No. V)

Woodwind Trio

MOZART

Bourrée

Woodwind Trio

KREBS

C Flute

Oboe or
2nd Flute

B♭
Clarinet

A i r

FABER

Menuetto

Woodwind Trio

HAYDN

D.C. al Fine

D.C. al Fine

D.C. al Fine

Allegro

Woodwind Trio

HANDEL

* Observe 𝅗 on repeat only.

Andante Grazioso

Woodwind Trio

HAYDN

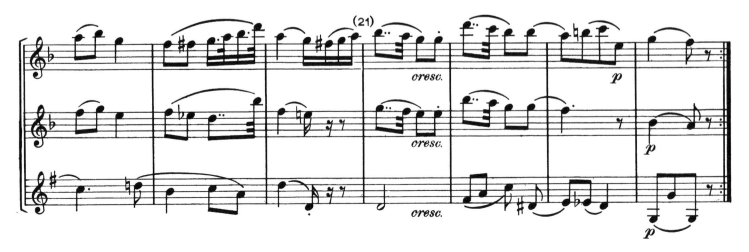

Menuetto
(Trio, Op. 87)

Woodwind Trio

BEETHOVEN

Woodwind Trio

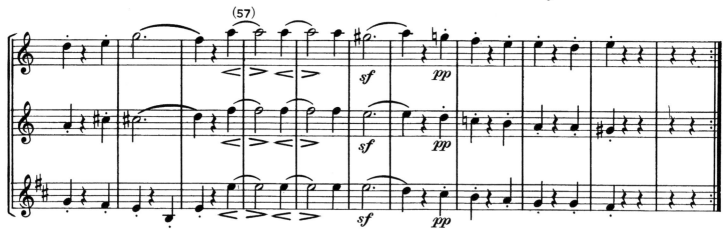

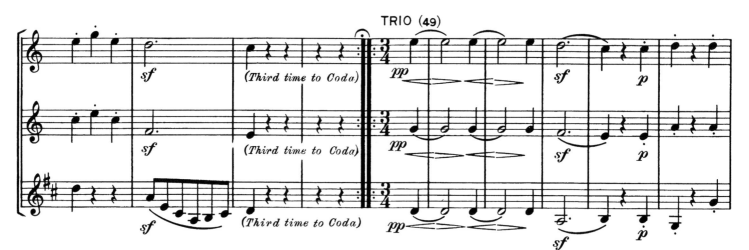

* *Menuetto da capo senza replica e poi Coda*

* *Menuetto da capo senza replica e poi Coda*

CODA

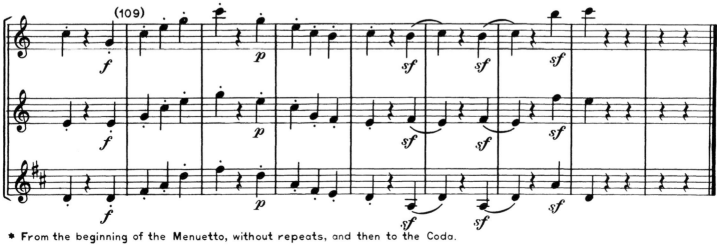

* From the beginning of the Menuetto, without repeats, and then to the Coda.

Two Dances

I - SARABANDE

Woodwind Trio

PAUL KOEPKE

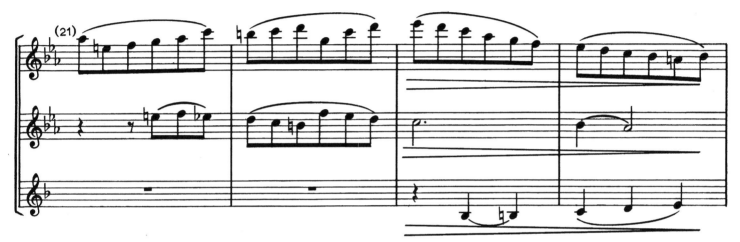

Woodwind Trio

II-BADINERIE

Arioso

Woodwind Trio

LEROY OSTRANSKY

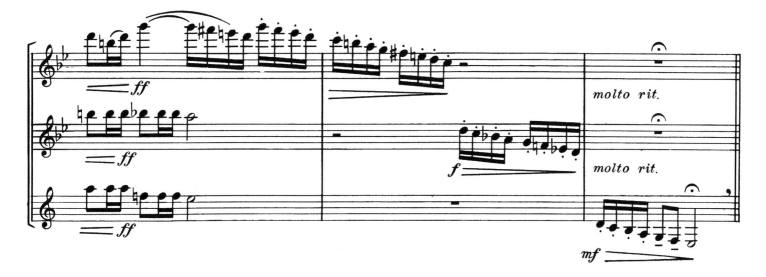

Larghetto
(Divertimento II)

Woodwind Trio

MOZART

C Flute

Oboe or
2nd Flute

B♭
Clarinet

Menuetto
(Divertimento II)

Woodwind Trio

MOZART

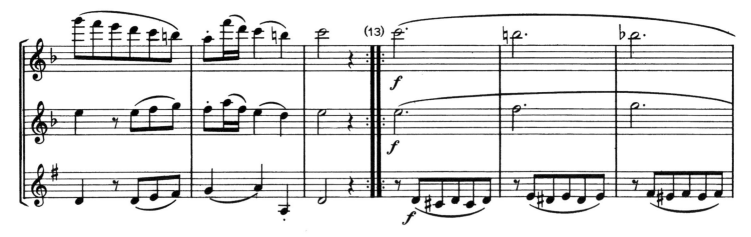

TRIO

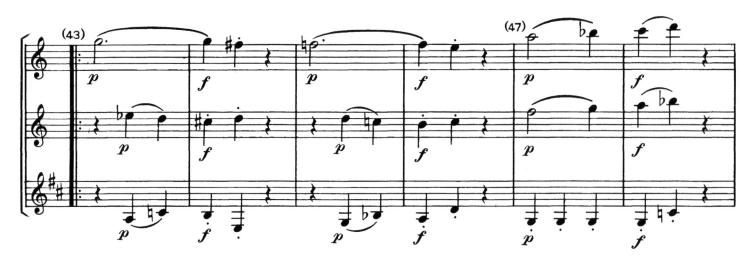

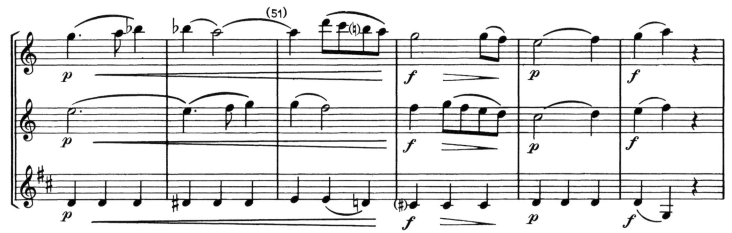

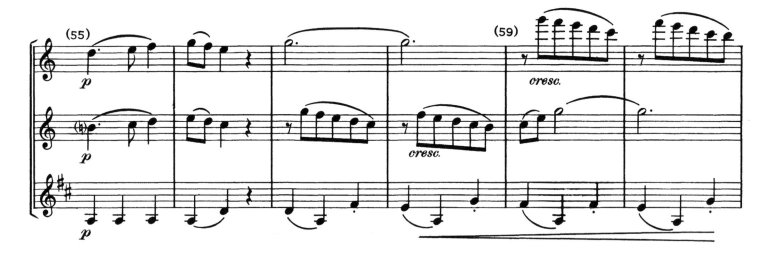

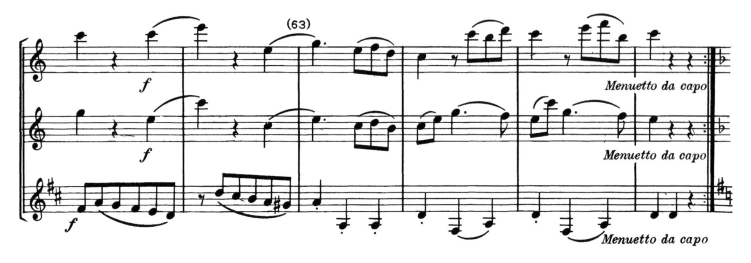